JERUSALEM, SHINING STILL

A CHARLOTTE ZOLOTOW BOOK

JERUSALEM, SHINING STILL

KARLA KUSKIN
ILLUSTRATIONS BY
DAVID FRAMPTON

A Charlotte Zolotow Book
HARPER & ROW, PUBLISHERS

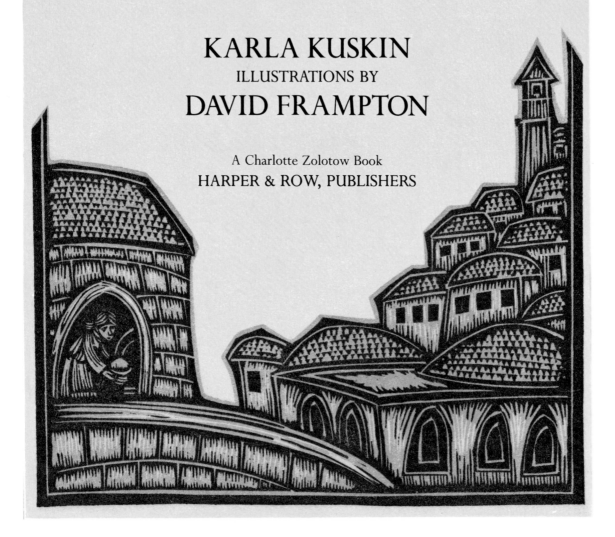

For Ruth
K.K.

Jerusalem, Shining Still

Text copyright © 1987 by Karla Kuskin

Illustrations copyright © 1987 by David Frampton

Printed in the U.S.A. All rights reserved.

10   9   8   7   6   5   4   3   2   1

First Edition

Library of Congress Cataloging-in-Publication Data

Kuskin, Karla.

Jerusalem, shining still.

"A Charlotte Zolotow book."

Summary: Evokes the spirit of an ancient city,
recalling David, Nebuchadnezzar, Herod, Hadrian,
Constantine, Saladin, Suleiman, and the many groups who
came to conquer; and observes that despite
3000 years of being battered, burned, and rebuilt,
Jerusalem shines peacefully in the moonlight.

1. Jerusalem—History—Juvenile literature.
[1. Jerusalem—History]   I. Frampton, David, ill.
II. Title.

DS109.9.K87   1987   959.94'4   86-25841

ISBN 0-06-023548-9

ISBN 0-06-023549-7 (lib. bdg.)

Thinking About Time

Think of a sunrise, a whole day, sunset and then night. That is a long time. Now think of three hundred and sixty-five sunrises, whole days, sunsets and nights with rain, with snow, with flowers or falling leaves, and you have thought of a year.

Now think about the city of Jerusalem. It has existed for four thousand years. For the first one thousand years it was so small and far away that hardly anyone knew anything about it. The first one thousand years. That is the first three hundred and sixty-five thousand days. Three hundred and sixty-five thousand sunrises and sunsets. That is season after season after season after season until you are bound to lose count. And four thousand years is four times as long as that. Let us just say that long ago, very long ago, very, very, long, long ago the story of this city began to begin.

The bread is baked before sunrise. I have seen a loaf that looks like a pair of eyeglasses. And another in the shape of a ladder. Every morning sixty-four kinds of bread are baked here. Every day in these narrow old streets seventy languages are spoken. This is not a very large city. It is far, far away from many that are much larger and newer. Then why should so many people come from everywhere to here? And why should they have been coming here for more than three thousand years?

Sit beside me. The sky is getting lighter. The sun comes up behind that ridge. It puts gold on the crescents and stars of the mosques, gold on the crosses of the churches. It touches the Western Wall and turns the old, enormous stones pure white. This is a city made of stone sitting along the tops of stony hills.

The hills have names. Mount Scopus, the Mount of Olives, Mount Zion over there across the way. King David is buried on Mount Zion. He has been in his tomb for three thousand years. Now he is dust, but once he was a boy. Then, on a morning just as clear as this one, just as white and blue, David walked into a valley not far from here and waited quietly as Goliath came toward him. Goliath the terrible. He was over nine feet tall. He wore a coat of knitted metal and a brass helmet. He carried a spear as high as a tree.

David was slim. He had no armor. He carried no spear. He put a smooth stone in his sling and let it fly. It hit Goliath, and all nine feet of him, and more, fell down stone dead. The valley trembled. Birds squawked and vanished. In the shaking sky clouds bumped against each other.

David went on winning battles. He won this city. It was very small, and there were walls around it. After the battle it was known as the City of David. Much later they began to call it Jerusalem.

David bought a high hill named Mount Moriah and put an altar there. Because he was a great king he wanted to have a great city. He knew that would take stones and time and something more. It would take countless men and women. Stonecutters cut rough blocks from the hills. They

loaded the stone on wooden sleds and donkeys' backs. The donkeys teetered down hills and scrambled over rocky ridges. They brought the stones to the city. Planners planned, draftsmen drew, and the workers worked the stone. They squared and finished it, lifted and set each separate block in place. The tapping of mallets on chisels, the rapping of chisels on stone echoed inside the city walls.

When King David died his son became king. King Solomon. He was famous for being wise. He knew one thousand and five songs by heart, and three thousand sayings. And while he sang his songs and said his sayings he kept the builders building.

They built walls and palaces and a great temple. A temple is a building like a church or a mosque, where people go to pray to the God they believe in. In the days of Solomon people believed in many gods. Gods of harvest, spring and fire. Gods of water, wine and love. But Solomon was a Jew, and the Jews have always believed in one God only. The temple was built to honor Him. It stood on Mount Moriah, the hill King David had bought. The temple stones glistened in the early morning. They glowed with gold in the afternoon, and under the faraway stars each stone was the color of moonlight.

Because the city was beautiful, kings fought for it. A king named Nebuchadnezzar conquered Jerusalem. He made the people his slaves and took them home with him to the country of Babylonia, where they wept. The city's walls and buildings were broken and brought down, streets were silent, and for fifty years the times were bad.

When times are bad they will get better. Babylonia fell to its enemies. The slaves were set free. Jerusalem had been torn down, but then new kings built it up again. It took seven years to finish the second temple, and for a long time it stood alone on Mount Moriah. Alone in the broken city. The workers went on working, and the city grew up slowly. Then times were good for one hundred years.

When times are good they will get worse. After the Babylonians had come from Babylonia, the Greeks came. They stole treasures from the temple and worshipped Greek gods there. The city was battered and burned. The Jews fled into the hills. They lived in caves and called themselves Maccabees. Maccabee means "hammer" in Hebrew. They hammered at the Greeks until they won the temple back, until they won the city back, until the building began again.

The tapping of mallets on chisels
the chipping of chisels on stone.
The placing and lifting and spacing and shifting
locking each block of rock
alone on its own.
Building a city of stone.

They built Jerusalem up, and then others tore it down again. After the Babylonians came from Babylonia, the Greeks came. And then came the Romans, those worshippers of gods and omens. They used stones and battering rams to break the walls and take the city. Their leader was Herod. He was famous as a murderer and a builder. He had the temple rebuilt. It was more beautiful than it had ever been. He ordered towers and then more towers and a palace with tremendous rooms that each held one hundred couches. There was some peace in the city for a while. Cats walked the walls, new flowers bloomed between old stones, lizards blinked their eyes and disappeared into the shadows.

Herod died. Not long after that a man whose name was
Jesus visited the city. He had been there many times when
he was a boy to listen to the wise men. As a man he came to
pray and preach. He cared about the poor, about people
who had been hurt by life. He had friends and followers
who loved him and enemies who hated him. One spring day
in Jerusalem Jesus was killed on a small hill called Golgotha,
a stony hill that looks like a skull. He was killed by his
enemies, but his friends kept his ideas alive. They kept his
name alive too. He came to be known as Jesus Christ.

The cruel, greedy Roman rulers got crueler and greedier. Once more the Romans and Jews went to war.

Their weapons were fire and arrows and stones
battering walls
shattering bones.
Murdering peace and the life that had been.
When men go to war very few of them win.

Thousands were dead and the city was left in ruins. The Romans who were still alive were the winners. Hadrian was the emperor then. He knocked down everything that was still standing and built a little Roman city there. Where the great temple had been, a Roman temple was put up in honor of Jupiter, king of the Roman gods. Only one wall of the old temple was left. That was the Western Wall. Even today Jews pray before that wall. But in those old days no Jews were allowed to enter the Roman city. For two hundred years there were bad times.

When times are bad they will get better. A Roman emperor named Constantine came to power. He was a Christian and he wanted to rebuild Jerusalem. He thought it should be a Christian city to honor Jesus Christ, who had died there. After the warriors were gone the quarrying went on.

They leveled and beveled and chiseled the stone.
Each rock and block of it
set on its own.
It was lifted and shifted
by women and men
who believed in Jerusalem
and built it again.

And when the new buildings rose, the Christian crosses on their roofs glistened over the city, under the sky.

Three hundred years passed, and the Persians came and took the city in twenty days. They killed Christians and burned their churches. The glistening crosses fell.

After the Persians, the Moslems came. They believed in one God, whose prophet was named Mohammed. And they believed that Mohammed had ridden a winged horse directly from Mount Moriah to Heaven. The Moslems, like the Christians and the Jews, thought that Jerusalem was a special place in the world, a holy city. Where the great temples had once stood they built two beautiful mosques on Mount Moriah. And everywhere they built new buildings with Moslem stars and crescents glistening on domed roofs over the city and under the sky.

New blossoms bloomed between old stones.
The streets were full of chants and chimes.
Cats sat like statues on white walls.
Such are the days in peaceful times.

You may remember that after the Babylonians came from Babylonia, the Greeks came. Then came the Romans, those worshippers of gods and omens. Then the Persians came in troops, the Moslems followed, groups and groups.

And then, more than one thousand years ago, the Fatimid Egyptians came to the city. They brought bad times and good times. Churches were burned down and built up again. The Seljuks from Turkey invaded. Earthquakes shook the hills and split the stone Mohammed's horse had stood upon before he and Mohammed flew to Heaven from Mount Moriah.

And then the Crusaders came to conquer. They were Christian soldiers. That means that they were followers of Jesus Christ. But Christ did not believe in killing, and the Crusaders did. They killed the Moslems and the Jews and ruled Jerusalem for eighty-seven years. During that time only Christians were allowed to live in the city. When the warriors departed the quarrying started.

Squaring and lifting and placing and shifting
stone upon stone against stone after stone.

Christian buildings rose. New churches and convents, new monasteries and hospices. And the Christian crosses on their roofs glistened over the city and under the sky.

Then a great Moslem warrior went to war against the Crusaders and captured the city. This was Saladin. He was powerful but not cruel. He protected the Christians and allowed the Jews to return.

Then there were more wars. More arrows, fire, spears and thrown stones. The Mameluke Egyptians took the city from Saladin. They were warriors and builders. Walls were raised, water was brought in from the hills and new stone domed buildings topped by glistening crescents and stars rose over the city and under the sky. In those days the Jews wore yellow turbans and the Christians wore blue. And the Mamelukes ruled for two hundred and sixty-seven years.

And then came the Ottoman Turks. Today an ottoman is a footstool but then it was an empire. The Ottoman Turks had a strong leader named Suleiman the Magnificent. To make new walls he commanded the

sledging and wedging and lifting and shifting
of stone against stone upon stone after stone.

The walls were white in the morning air.
They glowed with gold in the afternoon
and under the arc of the darkening sky
each stone was as pale and as cool as a moon.

Those are the walls you see today.

The rulers who came after Suleiman were not as magnificent as he had been. Some were dumb and some were dishonest and some were both. The city got poorer. And the country around the city got poorer. And the countries around the country around the city got poorer too.

You have not forgotten that after the Babylonians came from Babylonia, the Greeks came and then the Romans, those worshippers of Gods and omens. Then the Persians came in troops, Moslems followed, groups and groups, the Fatimid Egyptian forces, Seljuk Turks on foot and horses. After that the Crusaders, Saladin and more Moslems, the Mamelukes and the Ottoman Turks all came to stay, for a while, and went away.

And then, almost seventy years ago, the British came to Jerusalem. The city was so big by that time that it had spread beyond the city walls. Jews and Christians and Moslem Arabs lived in their own neighborhoods and worshipped in their holy places. When times were bad there was fighting between them, and when times were good there was peace.

When the British left the Jews and Arabs went to war. At last they stopped fighting and agreed on a truce that divided the city into two parts. Guns, sandbags, barbed wire and distrust separated one side from the other for twenty years. Then the two sides went to war again. The war lasted for six days. When it was over the barbed wire and the sandbags were taken away and the city was one city again.

Look at it across the valley. The sky is very dark and high, and the moon is hanging above Mount Zion by an invisible thread. Its light touches the stones of Golgotha and Mount Moriah. It puts gold on the crescents and stars of the mosques, gold on the crosses of the churches. It touches the Western Wall and turns the old, enormous stones pure white. For three thousand years this city has been battered and burned, and then built up, rebuilt and built again. Tonight, spreading across the tops of stony hills, it sits at peace beneath the moon. Three thousand years have passed, and still Jerusalem shines. King David would be proud.